How to be a Successful Forex Trader

Insider Tips for the Latest Internet Money-Making Sensation

By: Laura Evans

9781635014266

PUBLISHERS NOTES

Disclaimer – Speedy Publishing LLC

This book was originally printed before 2014. This is an adapted reprint by Speedy Publishing LLC with newly updated content designed to help readers with much more accurate and timely information and data.

Speedy Publishing LLC

40 E Main Street, Newark, Delaware, 19711

Contact Us: 1-888-248-4521

Website: http://www.speedypublishing.co

REPRINTED Paperback Edition: 9781635014266:

Manufactured in the United States of America

DEDICATION

To Martha – who has always been there for me.

TABLE OF CONTENTS

CHAPTER 1- UNDERSTANDING FOREX TRADING SECRETS

Forex trading involves dealing in international currencies. Here, one can sell currency of one country to buy that of another. The trader deals in Foreign Exchange [Forex] at the most appropriate time to profit from the transaction. Good ability to forecast plays a vital role here. One may wonder how Forex trading can be such a lucrative earning opportunity since fluctuations in exchange is so little. But remember, when done in big volumes, a minor change can mean a lot.

There are many nonmonetary advantages to it as well. Anyone who wants to deal in Forex can do so, since only the basic knowledge is required for it. Forex can help you earn a lot of money. But there are certain conditions to follow before trading in Forex. Firstly, one must have a thorough knowledge about the trends in the stock market, the basics of trading and risk-taking ability. You will get all the help you need for attaining these conditions very easily. There are many sites on the internet which can help you clarify your basics and help you brave rough weather.

A good reason why Forex trading can be considered is the fact that there are frequent fluctuations in currencies, though in percentage terms it may be small. You gain if the fluctuation favors you and the reverse holds true as well. No one can accurately predict the trend of the currencies. Liquidity is another reason why Forex trading is so popular. Now the most important part – in Forex, you can make huge sums of money even if your initial investment is on a lower side. You can invest as little as $50,000. Rich people have no upper cap to the amount of investment. So remember that even with a nominal investment, the earning ability is undoubtedly very huge.

Most of the great businesses are connected to the world of internet today, and Forex trading is no exception. You can deal in foreign currencies right from your home. In fact, it is fully conducted online. You have the liberty to choose when you want to trade, and you don't need to meet any deadlines. Basically, you can be your own boss.

The process of online trading is fairly simple for anyone to understand. You just need to open an account for Forex trading with a recognized broker and they will complete the rest of the formalities. The only bit you need to do is get ready with your investment amount. So, it is thus clear that Forex trading can be one of the best businesses to earn money. Though there is a level of risk attached to it, but it can be avoided with due care and an alert mind!

Why is Forex Trading Important?

Foreign Exchange [Forex] involves exchanging of different foreign currencies for a profit. The reason for buying the currency of another country may be the need to buy some commodity of the said country as well, besides making money through the difference in exchange rates. In the latter case, people buy currency of a foreign country when the rate in the market is low, and sell it off when the rates go up. Currency trading is usually done between the central banks, the government, speculators and MNCs. Nations cannot trade with each other without the presence of a foreign market.

A huge amount of money is daily traded in the Forex market, though the amount invested by an individual trader may be very low. No one individually can have any influence on the Forex fluctuations, not even the government. So it can easily be concluded that the level of the currency reflects the strength or the weakness of the economy of a country. So this makes the Forex market a good place for competition.

The government and the central bank do try to stabilize the currency of their country by speculating, by buying and selling currencies at appropriate times. So they can influence the market if they conduct a trade in huge volumes, though. To buy its own currency, however, the government or the central bank must have huge reserves of foreign currency with them. So it is virtually impossible to inflate the currency value artificially.

Banks trade a lot in foreign currencies and this forms a chunk of the volume in the Forex market. They buy currencies not only as individual bodies, but also on behalf of their clients. They trade in lots of futures. Till a few years back, the brokers could influence the volumes of trading in the Forex market. But due to the electronic services available now, the services of brokers is not required. It's easy to operate electronically. Trading with international countries is possible only with the existence of Forex markets. When there is no Forex market, there is no common currency between two countries, so one cannot evaluate the value of one currency with respect to the other.

The buyer pays the seller in the former's currency. With the money so received, the seller buys goods in the buyer's country and sells those goods in his [seller] country. Only then he is able to know how much he has earned through the export. In the presence of a Forex market, though, it is very easy for a seller to know of his earnings at the very instant that he conducts an export trade. In the same manner, the buyer too will have a thorough knowledge of the cost he will have to incur to buy goods from an international country.

What Makes Online Forex Trading Unique?

A few years ago, the Forex trading was limited mainly to gigantic money center banks and other financial institutional traders. But, in the recent years, new technological innovations and development of the online trading software, like the one used by FX, permit several small forex traders to take the benefits of currency trading with the foreign exchange.

Initially, when the era of Forex trading began, only the big enterprises could access the forex trading countenance in the inter-bank business within the world. However, quite recently the forex market has become more accessible to the private clients. Most of the people thing as earning money in Forex market is very easy but it is very tough. Lacks and lacks of people come regularly to this market but very few out of them can able to earn money and stay for the longer time.

There is no process defined to success in the Forex market. But the basics of Forex market are defined and one must try to follow it to maximize the probability of success in the Forex market. One has to plan his entry to this market. You must know Forex market very well. You must go through one of the Forex market course. You must have practice through Forex market dummy accounts. You must get the best Forex software that suits your requirements of Forex market. You must take the help of the experts in the form of Forex market alerts or Forex market technical analysis techniques for your trade in Forex market.

All of these points will be explained in coming chapter so that you can make your entry counted. The online forex trading permits an individual to open an account and profitably invest in several types of foreign currencies through the Internet. The online forex trader is provided with software, which gives him the ability to manage the trading account with a Multilanguage facility, besides the other tools and analysis that makes investing money an easy and profitable job.

The online forex trader provides a protected environment for the investors or company who opts to carry out the online forex trading. To be able to operate the software in this protected environment, the investor needs to have a computer system and Internet connection that will effectively run the forex software without any glitch.

Chapter 2- A Discussion on Which Currencies to Trade and Which to Avoid

When it all comes down to it, there are many types of currency trades out there in the Forex market. If you are considering an investment into Forex, you need to start out where the funds are most likely to occur. Many Forex investors who are new to the process put too much of their focus on the currencies that they believe are the best, such as rare or unknown currencies. This can lead to problems because of the amount of volatility and the lack of liquidity in the market place. Therefore, it is a better option for you to stick with some of the more well-known currencies if you hope to make a profit right out of the door.

There are no currencies in the world that you absolutely should stay away from, however that changes often. If you are new to the world of Forex trading, however, you do want to stay away from currencies that pair exotic or uncommon currency pairs together. It is often best to select those pairs that trade most often since this is where you will find the largest opportunity for profit, anyway. Any novice Forex trader who dabbles in exotic currencies or those pairs that are simply uncommon are likely to find themselves losing money.

Which Currencies Should You First Trade With?

If you do not want to dabble in the major currency pairs just yet (which include the EUR/USD, GBP/USD, USD/JPY) then you need to focus on those pairs that are more common or at least that are easier for beginners to get into. This includes any of the following currencies:

• Euro (EUR)

• British Pound (GBP)

• United States Dollar (USD)

• Swiss Franc (CHF)

• Japanese Yen (JPY)

• Australian Dollar (AUD)

• Canadian Dollar (CAD)

Some great pairs that happen here and it does not have to take a lot of expertise to do well. If you are looking at any other pairs, look for those that do not have high spreads. It is important to note that spreads will vary from one broker to another broker, though, so doing basic research is important before you start investing. You can gather all the information you need from a broker's website or from the trading platform itself, if you would like. The key is to make safer decisions until you get the experience.

Tips on Currency Pairing for the Beginners

As you start your Forex career, or even if you are just testing the waters, you will want to focus on pairs that can provide you with the highest amount of profit without being as risky as some others are. The key is to know what your options are and to know which pairs of currencies are the best to focus on. With many different pairs out there in currency, it is easy to get overwhelmed and confused, long before you actually find yourself making a profit. For this reason, it is best to stick with the following three pairs because they provide the best results for most people.

EUR/USD

The euro to United States Dollar is the best combination and it is the most popular pair for most people. It has the lowest spread that you will find in any currency trading. It responds well to basic technical studies of Forex, unlike some other forms, and this makes it easier for those who are new to Forex to learn how the system works. Under normal circumstances in the market, the EUR/USD pair is not necessarily volatile, unless there is some type of reason for this. More so, it has a strong global view and it is covered extensively. All of this equates to less risk and closer stops.

USD/JPY

The combination of the Yen and the Dollar is often a good one for beginners as well. Here, you have about the same low spread as you do with the EUR/USD. This makes it a great choice for any investor. Second, it offers smoother trends and when you compare it to other pairs, this makes a significant different.

GBP/USD

The final match up for beginners is the Great Brittan Pound to the Dollar. This pair moves largely and it can bring more pips in one simple move than either of the other two mentioned transactions. This is the pair to consider for breakout trading. However, there are risks associated with this pairing that need to be noted. You will need further away place stops and the pair can be quite volatile.

If you stick with these three pairs, you will find your inexperience with Forex trading is not nearly as hard to overcome as if you were using other trading methods. It is very important to focus on the types of trades that offer some level of risk protection when you are new to trading.

Chapter 3- Defining the 4 Order Types in the Forex Market

There are many kinds of orders which traders can place to transact in the Forex market, for making profit out of it.

•Market Order The market order is the most simple and common kind or order. Here, the trader buys and sells the currency at the rate prevailing in the market at the time of placing the order. Due to the huge size of the market and the high volatility, trends can reverse any instant, so people prefer placing orders at the market price to guard them against any adverse trend.

•Limit order. In this case, the trader specifies a price at which he may wish to buy or sell the currency. Suppose a trader has bought GBP against the USD at 1.9710, then he can place a sell order at

1.9725, when the exchange will execute the order and he will profit from it. The order will get cancelled if the target price is not achieved during the day.

•Stop loss order. Due to the volatility, stop losses are essential. They determine the maximum loss a trader is willing to suffer. Suppose in the above instance, the risk-taking ability of the trader is low, then he may place a stop loss at 1.9705, at which level the exchange will book losses for him, and he won't be affected by any fall below 1.9705.

•Entry order. Such an order is filled only when certain conditions are met in the market, which the order specifies. The entry order can be a limit entry order or even a stop entry order.

– Limit entry order. As an example, let's assume that the current market price for GBP/USD is 1.9705-10. This implies that the trader can transact at these levels. Here, a trader can put a limit entry order to sell his holdings at a price more than the market price, say, 1.9715. His order would be executed only if that price is attained. In the similar manner, he can place an order for buying at a level of, say 1.9700, and his 'buy' order would remain pending till the price falls to that level.

- Stop entry order. Such an order is generally used when the trader has sufficient grounds to believe that the currency is trading in a fixed range and believes that it is on the verge of a breakout from that range. He might want to buy at a price higher than the market price or sell at a lower price than the market price. In the same example, the trader may go ahead and buy at 1.9720 or sell at 1.9690, where he believes that once these levels are attained, the currency will only go up or fall further, as the case may be. A trader exercises the stop entry order only when a trader has reasonable grounds to believe that there will be sharp movements in the currency rates in the Forex market

CHAPTER 4- STUDY MARKET TRENDS TO PROFIT

Understanding expense trends of Forex is not easy at all. Businessmen often get wrong ideas and make agendas based on them and suffer losses. The following can help you understand the trends:

You predict the Forex expense trends Businessmen observe a certain level and jumps on to it thinking that it's stable. However, this is simply based on assumption and that never works in Forex business. There is no accurate prediction. If wining is the goal, you have to base the business on the sure shot expense trends. Related to this, there are certain factors given below.

The Scientific Laws Used by Markets

There is a notion, which believes that market trends are based on logic. Some believers are Gann, Elliot and the followers of Fibonacci. However, if everybody knew everything, prices would never have been a surprise and markets would be non-existent.

The layman would accept these ideas and their fantastic suggestions. However facts say otherwise.

How Trends Occur

It is not advisable as news is actually insignificant. The way news is supposed is what decides the movements. Let's see how trends occur.

Actual Expense Trends

Basics + Individual Insight into them = Forex Market Trends People are seldom rational. They often function emotionally, which is why logical reasoning does not always hold true. The real human psychology is consistent but these matters have no logic: 1. People make costs move to extreme and these passing points can be used profitably. 2. Carry on with business. Don't get into guessing.

Win the Competition

Forex is a sport and competition is based on chances. You may not be able to determine chances but you will never lose. That applies not for every instance but try out on big probability situations and you will surely take the cake with very few losses. Get huge proceeds in due course of time. Voracity and panic changes costs while creating points that are visible on Forex schedules can be used gainfully. It's a game so when prices fluctuate on your side, get to business. Control your finances well and be a winner.

Be Imperfect but Never a Loser

Forex markets teem with those who attempt guessing and try to get a non-existent undisclosed trend cipher. Even though Forex expense trends seem disordered, basing your business on cost fluctuations will make you a winner. It may not be an ideal business for many, however if done right, you can make a lot of money through forex trading.

CHAPTER 5- HOW ONLINE FOREX TRADING REVOLUTIONIZED THE HOME-BASED INTERNET BUSINESS

Work from home trend is increasing rapidly. For the past few years the Internet business has taken wide steps and opened different opportunities for home based business. Forex trading is the boom to this industry. If you are one of them who works from home and looking for the new opportunities then be ready to learn the art of forex trading - new revolution to home based Internet business.

Forex trading is an online business. People can conduct their trade from wherever and whenever they want as this is also the 24X7 market. Now a day, the number of people working from home is increasing rapidly and forex trading opens the real doors for regular good income to this segment of people. People just need PC with Internet connection, forex trading software, and knowledge about the forex market to start the trading in the forex market.

You need to understand the forex market and its different shares to get success in the forex market. This can be done by gathering information related to forex market, getting the forex courses, getting the right forex software, and following the best forex signals to conduct the trade in the forex market.

Forex market provides you the opportunity of regular income with all the benefits of business. If you want to work full time from your home and want to earn money out of the forex market then you must go through one of the forex course. It will help you understand the forex market better and rip the benefits at its best.

Forex software plays very important role in the success of your forex home based Internet business. You must choose the right forex software for your forex market trades. The best thing about the forex home based Internet business in compare to other home based business is that you don't need to depend upon others to pay for your work. Here you will work and you are going to be paid instantly. You don't need to wait for the payments for your service. You don't need to depend upon others for your income.

Starting Forex Trading At Home

With the advent of internet the forex trading market has become online forex trading market. Every day hundreds of new forex traders get registered for the online forex accounts to try their luck in the online forex trading. Most of the new forex trades come with a predefined belief that they can make huge amounts of wealth though online forex trading, but this is not true. In this type of trading system the forex traders are in control of how much they can lose or win. An impulsive and hasty decision can make the forex trader lose more than he can earn.

How to be a Successful Forex Trader

Requirements to start forex trading as home based Internet business:

You must have place at your home where you can establish your work station, which is nothing but a PC with Internet connection.

You must have knowledge about the forex trading market. It is always advisable to depend upon yourself then on others for your forex trade. Collect as much information as you can about the forex market from internet and other social Medias available to you.

Once you have your own knowledge about the forex market, it is time to get experts courses. Search for forex trading courses available to you through internet as well through your local contact and opt for the best. After completing these two steps you will get the basic as well as the technical knowledge about the forex trading market.

Now it is the time to test your knowledge and for testing forex trading knowledge you can take the help of dummy forex trading accounts. Dummy forex trading accounts are the accounts similar to the forex regular accounts. The only difference is that here there is no flow of real money. You can do as much trades as you like and test your skills in every possible level with every risk degrees.

Once you feel confident that now you can step in to this forex trading market it is time to get the best forex trading software for you. There are many websites that offer forex trading software. It can be a tough choice to decide which the best among them is. You can take advice from your friends, relatives, and colleagues to find out the forex software that suits your needs. Analyze the benefits offered by the forex software properly, it should be able to offer you the best and be easy to understand too.

Forex alerts are the best tools to get advice from the forex experts and conduct trade accordingly to increase the chances of getting profit out of the forex market.

Why Objectivity is Essential in Forex Trading

It is difficult for Forex traders to realize that the currency market is extremely unpredictable. As new traders spend a long time trying to learn the mechanics of the foreign exchange trade and focus their time and energy on trying to find a method for predicting movements, they naturally expect there to be rules governing the movement of the market. This not being the case, many traders find themselves at a disadvantage.

While Forex traders have a number of tools at their disposal, which allow them to judge the right time to open or close a position, many prefer to rely mostly on one tool. So, having opened a position, they watch their favorite indicator and, to a large extent, base their trading decisions solely on it, ignoring the others. This works well enough until that indicator starts telling them something different from what the others are. Traders caught in an open position which their favorite tool is telling them to hold, will often do so, despite the fact that other tools are telling them to close and get off the market, and end up losing money.

The basic problem, of course, is that the trader is not looking at the market as is, but through the lenses of his own expectations about it and further using his favorite indicator to reinforce those ideas instead of looking at the bigger picture. And, encouraged by the fact that his chosen indicator is forecasting the profit he wants, the trader is focusing more on money than on the market. If the Forex market was not unpredictable, it would collapse because all traders would profit all the time. There are many tools that can help traders predict the direction of the market and they usually do an efficient job. But even in the hands of the most experienced traders, the best tools occasionally fail to predict the market's movements correctly.

Losing in trade because of predicting the market wrongly is an innate part of Forex trading and traders need to accept it. Besides, they need to learn to avoid getting in a position where they do not have many choices. For this, the trader needs to accept the fact that the foreign exchange market pretty much has a mind of its own and the traders have to follow its movements instead of trying to make it go in the direction they want it to.

CHAPTER 6- DIFFERENTIATING THE TYPES OF FOREX ACCOUNTS

A beginner has three options. You can either jump straight in the live real trade with a standard account. You may have to invest something in between $1,000 and $5,000. This could be very risky for the starters as the forex trading market is uncertain. Thus, you must not opt for this unless you have gained too much of experience in forex trading through some source.

Secondly, you can start doing your live trading with the use of real money, but it is recommended that you use the mini forex trading account. There are many brokers in the market who ask the beginners to make a low investment of just $250 to get started. If you search around a little then you may find brokers who agree to start forex trading with even less amount of money.

Last, but the most convenient option for the forex traders is that they use the forex demo account to get started. Through forex demo account method, you can learn about the real methods of the forex trading market without yourself risking any money. The main idea behind the use of forex demo account in trading is that you can practice the art using this and then move on to the live trading, which you can start by switching off with a mini trading account or a standard account.

Forex Demo Account vs. Mini Forex Trading

If you are beginner in the forex trading business then you may first need to look around for a good forex demo account. It contains several advantages that are especially tailor made for the beginners. Apart from this, there is also the mini forex trading account. Are you confused about which is better than the other? Then let us find out whether a forex demo account is preferable or you must go with the mini forex trading account.

A mini trading account is specially designed for those who are learners in the forex trading business. This account allows you to trade in the real market with real money, but in very small amount so that you don't incur huge losses. This account can be easily opened with a small amount of starting fund. There are many brokers who can offer you a mini forex trading account which is one tenth of the standard account that is usually used for trading.

Most of the beginners opt for the last option, the forex demo account, because in their opinion it is safer to use the 'pretend money' than to start trading online with real money. A forex demo account also gives you enough freedom to try out different strategies and systems. However it is recommended that you stick to just one system while using the forex demo account. The only disadvantage in the forex demo account is that, you know that it is not real and this inspires you to take hasty and risky decisions which may not be suitable for real forex trading market. This would make you uncomfortable when you are in the real forex trading market. So, choose forex demo account at the beginning but then sharpen your skills using a mini forex trading account.

Mini Forex Account vs. Regular Forex Account

If you are new to this place then it is always suggested to get one forex mini account and try your luck in this market or if you have experience in the forex market then you must go for forex regular account.

The main difference between the forex mini account and forex regular account is that, in case of forex mini account - you are allowed to open an account with just $250 where as in the case of forex regular account it is $2000 to $2,500. The initial account opening amount may vary from broker to broker. Due to the tough competition market some brokers open forex mini account for $25 only. This also helps to increase the number of traders in the market. But, it is completely depends upon the brokers through which you open your account. In case of forex regular account you trade currency in lots of 100,000, where as in forex mini account it is 10,000. Trading currency in lots is rather confusing. This is just to know the difference between the two.

The main advantage of opening a forex mini account instead of forex regular account is that you are decreasing your changes of losing heavy amount in trades. As every trade happens in lots and points, if you invest your money for higher lots or points, the result may either get you huge profit or huge lose. For general if you lost 10% of your investment, then in the forex mini account you lose will be $25 (10% of $250) where as in case of forex regular account it is $200 (10 % of $2000), which shows more loss of money in case of forex regular account. So, as a beginner, it is also advisable to start with forex mini account instead for going with forex regular account.

Trading in Lots

As a beginner to Forex trading, you may find yourself confused about the term lots. In Forex, the currencies are traded in lots. The standard size for a lot is 100,000 units. The unit is the base currency that is being traded. The best way to understand how this occurs is to look at an example. If you are using the cross USD/CHF, for example, the base currency here is the USD. This means that the trade may be one standard lot of USD/CHF, which would be worth $100,000. Consider another example of this. If you were using the cross GBP/USD, then the base currency here is the GBP. This means that one lot would be worth 100,000 pounds.

If this is confusing simply look at a few more examples of it before you move on. However, it is also important to note that not all of the lots traded in Forex are for standard lots. In fact, many of the trades that occur are for different amounts. The same principle and set up still applies, though. You can trade by a two of three types of lots that you can trade by, or sizes. The standard lot, as mentioned, is 100,000 units of the base currency. A mini lot is equal to 10,000 units of the base currency. Then there are also micro lots, which are equal to 1,000 units of the base currency.

As you get started in Forex trading, do note that the type of account you have plays a role in the lots that you can purchase. Those who open mini accounts will have access to mini and micro lots. These are people that open the account with any place between $200 and $1000. Those who want to trade in standard lot sizes will need to open a larger account only. Also, note that the size requirements for opening a standard account will change based on the broker that you are working with.

What does all of this mean to you as a trader, though? In short, the smaller the lot size is, the lower the profits will be. At the same time, if you do not invest as much, chances are good that you will lose less money as well. Finding the right balance here really comes down to understanding the risks that you can take on. As a beginner, a lower risk level is often a good decision.

Easier Forex Trading Profits with the Right Tools

There is no one single super smart Forex trading tool which gives you profit, profit and more profit. The only possible solution is to use a combination of different tools to identify the favorable market forces to get a maximum number of high probability trades over a period of time. Trend lines are the most popular and reliable Forex trading tool which many successful traders give their testimonial for.

The Three Trend line Strategy

Trend Lines are an important tool for trend identification and confirmation in technical analysis. It is a straight line that connects two or more price points and then extends into the future to guide you. There will be lines drawn across significant lows in an uptrend, and significant highs in a downtrend. To roughly classify trend lines, we can divide them into three as short term trend lines, medium term trend lines and long term trend lines.

1. Short Term Trend lines

Draw these lines across the most recent two lows for an uptrend or across most recent two highs for a downtrend. Best observations are found on a smaller time frame such as a 15 minute or 30 minute chart.

2. Medium Term Trend lines

These are best observed on a higher time frame like a 60 minute chart. It either connects the nearest significant low to current price action to the previous significant low in an uptrend or the nearest significant high to current price action to the previous significant high in a downtrend.

3. Long Term Trend lines

It uses higher time frames such as the 4 hour chart or the daily chart to draw long term trend lines using the same method of Medium Term Trend lines. The long term trend line is considered as an effective Forex trading tool. The daily chart is used mostly by traders of big institutions who do not usually engage in small moves on an intraday level.

By drawing a trend line on a daily chart you can graphically analyze where price is and where it is likely to bounce. But employ trend lines as a Forex trading tool with caution and discretion. Covering your charts with every trend line possible will result in confusion and blurry analysis. It is not a good idea to rely completely on a short time trend line. They merely give you a defined picture of current price action. These are broken often during the course of a day. Their main use is to give you a clear, instantly recognizable graphical representation of current price behavior.

If you notice price coming back to test a trend line on the higher time frames, look at other factors. Draw in horizontal lines to mark key support and resistance using previous highs and lows. Draw Fibonacci retracement and extension levels. Calculate the daily pivot points and put them on your chart. Have the 200 EMA (Exponential Moving Average) shown on your charts.

CHAPTER 7- HOW TO OPEN AN ONLINE FOREX TRADING ACCOUNT

With the advancement of the World Wide Web, everything in the world has shrunk and come into a nutshell. Even Forex market is no exception. Today, you can easily open a forex trading account through simple steps, by just the click of your mouse. You can consult with online forex trading brokers and get the best forex trading account for you sitting cozily at your home and become online forex trader. Here are the simple steps about opening an online forex trading account explained:

- Choose the type of online forex trading account that you wish to open
- Get yourself registered as online forex trader
- Activate your online forex trading accounts to get started your career as online forex trader Which Online Currency Should You Use?

Being an online forex trader, you can either get the forex trading account opened in your name or in the name of your business. There are also a wide variety of options available such as a standard or a mini currency trading account. The forex trading account is just like a brokerage account that is used by the online forex trader who is just a beginner in the forex market. Those who are new to trading are recommended to open the mini currency trading account for all transactions. The mini account allows the online forex trader to take smaller position in a currency; instead of the trading through standard accounts that is mostly used by regular online forex traders.

Usually in a 'forex mini account', the online forex trader is allowed to trade in agreement size of 10,000 units, in the place of the standard 100,000. The forex standard forex trading accounts are usually for the regular and experienced online forex traders. Completing Registration Families You need to follow certain formalities in order to get registered and get a forex trading account. The account opening formalities may differ from one online forex trading broker to the other. Most of the online forex trading brokers hands over the trading account opening application forms to the traders in PDF format. The information that is asked for in the forms is generally very basic and can be easily provided.

Activating Your Account

After you submit all the required forex trading account opening documents to your online forex trading broker, you will get notified by an email. After receiving the email, you may need to complete several other formalities online, in order to get your forex trading account activated. Once, all the formalities are over, your online forex trading broker will send you all the details of forex trading account through mail. The details contain instructions, username, and password to start acting as online forex trader.

Which Trading Software is Best?

As currency trading market is an online trading business and all your transactions carried out online, you require online secure and reliable software to conduct all your currency trading requirements, which is nothing but the requirement of currency trading systems for your currency trading market.

Currency trading systems are the platforms where you conduct your trade. The better currency trading system you have, the better result you can expect. Currency trading systems play very vital role in the success of your currency trading career. You can get many currency trading systems from different sources like free online currency trading systems, paid online currency trading systems, from your local market, from your broker or even from the experts of the currency trading market. Source can be anywhere as long as the currency trading systems are reliable, secure, and suit your trading style and requirements.

Different currency trading systems are available as per your currency trading requirements, like if you are a full time currency trader then more manual permissions are given to you to perform the currency trading activities, where as in case of part time traders more automatic currency trading systems are offered to the service to save their time and provide best results out from each trade in the currency trading market.

Popularity of automated currency trading systems is increase very rapidly with the best success rates in the currency trading market. Now people prefer more automated currency trading systems over the regular currency trading systems for their currency trading activities in the currency trading market.

CHAPTER 8- CHOOSING THE RIGHT FOREX TRADING SYSTEM

When it comes to getting yourself into Forex trading, one thing you may be wondering about is the Forex trading systems that are out there. There are plenty of options to select from and even more opinions on if you should use them, how you should use them and which ones to use. Before you can make a decision about this, you should consider what the trading system can actually offer to you and why it may or may not be the best option for your particular needs. Some systems are not doubt better than others.

There are many systems out there and some of them are definitely going to be a better option than others are. The key here is not to buy a system or use a free one, based solely on that factor but to know what to look for. The first thing you need to consider is that the trading system needs to work with your own style of play. In other words, no matter if you are a long term swing trader or if you are a short term day trader, the system needs to work for your particular goals and your particular needs as such.

Next, consider how the Forex trading system addresses clear entry and exit signals. No matter which system you invest in, it is critical that you know that the system has these types of signals and that they work perfectly. If this is in place, this means there is no chance for your emotions to come into your trading. You want there to be 100 percent mechanical rules in place to protect you so that you do not make bad decisions at the wrong moment.

In addition, there should be some set of defined rules on stop loss size and placement. Many trading systems you will find out there do promise to provide you with high returns. They may or may not be able to deliver on this promise. If they are going to deliver they need to have good money management rules in place. You want there to be a stop loss placement so that you can avoid seeing your trading capital erased too fast based on just a few trades.

Although you do not have to have a Forex trading system, there is no reason not to have one if you select the right one to use in your trading.

Adding Forex Trading to Your Daily Business

There are many benefits to making the Forex market part of your daily business. This is a place where you will make a good deal of money, if you have taken the time to learn the ins and the outs of the business. It is a great place for you to build your wealth, for whatever goals you may have. Yet, many people find that Forex trading is a better option than traditional stop markets because Forex trading is available for such extensive hours of operation. No matter which way you look at it, Forex is the place you want to be to make money.

As long as you have the time, Forex is available to you. It does not operate on the weekends, like most businesses around the world do not. However, the business is available throughout the day and the night most other days of the week. For example, the Forex market trades 24 hours per day, every day during the week. The actual hours of operation are from Sunday evening at 20:000 GMT throughout to Friday evening at 22:00 GMT. This gives you all of the hours that you need to operate your trading plans.

It can also lead to burn out. Although most people do use automate systems to help them to monitor their Forex trading, it is not a good idea to spend too much time relying on those systems. You do need to have a hand in the actual transactions if you hope to turn a profit in them by watching the changes in the market place. Keep in mind that there are many different ways that you can change things within your transactions if the market changes directions or you learn of a new opportunity. If you leave everything on autopilot, you will miss out on these options.

On the other hand, you do not want to go to the extreme and try to trade all the time. Your mental sharpness will wear down, leading to mistakes and losses that were avoidable. In any case, the Forex market offers an ideal advantage by being open 24 hours a day. Even if there is significant breaking news occurring in the middle of the night, you can jump on to your trading market and make changes. This will improve the overall success of your trades, since you can make adjustments whenever you determine it is necessary to.

No-Commission Trading

There are outstanding benefits for trading on the Forex market as opposed to trading in other markets. You like the flexibility of being able to log into your account and make trades in the middle of the night, for example. You may also love the fact that you have great liquidity in the market. You can make changes to your Forex trading model when you need to, without having to worry about the actual length of time that your funds will be out of reach. However, it is also a good idea to consider Forex trading as a means of trading without having to pay excessive fees to do so.

What Commission?

Forex trading also allows you to trade the currencies without having to pay sizable commissions when you do so. This is one of the best reasons for you to invest in Forex. After all, who doesn't want to get to make money without having to pay expensive fees to do so? There are no commissions that need paid through trading forex. However, if you decide to work through a broker or other agent who will handle your trading, those services will require you to pay a price to use those services. This is not something that you have to do, though, and that makes Forex trading even more attractive than other types of trading.

If you have been burned by the stock market because of these downsides, you may be looking at the Forex market with skepticisms. The fact is currency trading does not have to be expensive to do so. It is important to note that there could be minor fees associated with the transaction.

If you are trading in the majors, you may find that it is even cheaper to trade on this market. The Majors are the most often traded currencies, including EURUSD, GBPUSD, USDCHF and the USDJPY. In other words, if you are trading in these markets, you will pay even less for doing the exchange. This is one of the many reasons so many people turn to the majors for their investing needs.

There are many reasons for you to invest in Forex trading, but not having to pay commissions has to be one of the top reasons so many people turn to this type of trading over other types. It is a good idea for you to invest in this method after you learn about the benefits.

CHAPTER 9- GETTING RICH THROUGH FOREX

Forex, Forex market, forex trading market, foreign market or foreign exchange market are the different names of money market, where traders trade with money. Means they buy and sell currencies in forex trading market. It is also known as currency market or currency exchange market. Earning money in this forex trading market is as easy as losing it. One has to be very careful while dealing with these types of trades. There are many important points, which can help you to make good profits and at times avoid you to fall in great loses.

- Proper training through good forex courses
- Sound practice through dummy accounts
- Starting trade through mini forex accounts
- Getting the right forex exchange broker for your trades
- Getting the right software for regular trading account

- Getting reliable and trusted forex trading alerts for your trades
- Use of forex charts for your trade

In which the first five points are followed by all the traders in the forex market. But, very few of them also follow the last two points to maximize the income in forex market.

Using Forex Alerts

Forex alerts are the tips or advices from the experts to what to do and what to not in this vast and volatile market. You can get these forex trading signals either in form of short messages to your mobile or short emails to your email Id. As these are the alerts, which have just a life of very short time, so you have to react very fast to earn the real profits out of it. Other important point is that the source of these forex alerts must be trustworthy. Otherwise you can end up with huge loses. Forex alerts are one of the best ways to maximize your earning in forex trading market. Good forex alerts provide you chances to maximize your profits in forex trading market.

Using Forex Charts

Forex trade market is difficult to understand and comprehend at one time. This is mainly because it keeps changing all the time and there are several factors which change and determine its moves. It is not possible for a forex trader to analyze and effectively take steps in the forex trade market. There are several tools available that help to analyze and comprehend the forex trade market, and one of the most important among them is the forex charts. In order to effectively make use of the forex charts, it is important for the trader to do the following:

-   Choose the right type of forex chart
-   Understand the forex charts correctly and
-   Act in proper manner on the basis of the forex charts indications

Do You Need a Forex Broker?

As you consider investing in Forex trading, one of the decisions you may want to make is to hire a financial broker who is experienced in Forex to handle the process for you. This is one of the best resources you will find out there since they have the skill, experience and time to manage the financial decisions you need to make if you are going to be profitable online. However, it is going to be up to you to tackle the Forex industry on your own. You do not want to hire just any broker out there. You may not even need one if you are experienced and do have the time necessary to devote to this process.

A Forex broker can manage your investments to the level that you want them to. For example, this may mean that they can handle the extensive decisions that have to be made on a regular basis. This may also mean that the Forex broker is able to offer advice to you on how you should invest, so that you do not have to do all of the research yourself. On the other hand, you may need to hire a financial broker to manage only certain things for you. You may want to make the decisions and just use a broker to perform the tasks you have stated. The level of use is up to you.

If you do decide you need a Forex broker, you need to hire the right person for the job. Hire a professional who has years of experience in the Forex markets. It is important to note that this is not just any type of investment history. They need to have Forex experience. In addition, you want to ensure that they have a long term experience. If they are just starting out, they have not noticed the ups and downs in the market place. Ask them about their record of accomplishment, fees, and of course how easy it will be for you to get in touch with them when you need to.

Hiring a Forex broker is necessary for most people. They provide services that you cannot pass up in most situations. More so, a broker is going to be able to provide you with the resources that you need to do well in the industry so that you do not have to spend your days analyzing the markets.

Tapping the Greatest Global Trade

Forex system happens to be the greatest global trade. It taps into some movements for businessmen to gain well. One accepted Forex business agenda utilized rather gainfully in the business is called Channel Breakout.

Forex Trading Channels – Channels consist of paths made on a schedule to trace the array where exchange had been transacted in a time span. They can be simply constructed. Observe the schedule in a time span and draw lines linking the comparatively tall spot business expenses, and down under linking a comparative low spot business expenses. This will give you a picture of the business array existent during a time span like, six months.

Channel Breakout – Once the value of exchange goes up the peak network line, there is a rising network getaway. Also, once the value goes down below the lowest network spot, you get a downward network getaway. Network getaways happen upwards and downwards. With enough Forex input with scientific scrutiny, everyone may utilize the process for getting a gainful exchange business agenda.

How to be a Successful Forex Trader

You have to build the channels very carefully. Every meeting of lines doesn't indicate a proper getaway. If there is any fallacy in the line construction, what you observe is business out of the array, which just leads you back inside. Therefore, before anything else, gain enough knowledge on Forex.

Gainful Control of Forex channels – When you figure out the working of networks, gains will happen. Construct the business with enough pauses. Then, in case of an incorrect getaway sign, you will get tolerable losses or if luck favors you, a very low profit.

But if you are on the correct side of a proper network getaway, the tiny lack you received will be moved away and you get a good big satisfactory gain. Any proper Forex business shareholder worth his name capitalizes on channel breakouts. In case you want to cash in the exchange markets, take out a certain amount of time for a Forex education to build this agenda and various technological scrutiny processes. That will build up the exchange agendas, which would yield gainful consequences. If you don't give some time to completely figure out the stakes and yields contained in a Forex business agenda, you may not get the desirable consequences. So you see your gain just depends on you.

CHAPTER 10- STEP-BY-STEP SECRETS TO SUCCESS

When 95% of traders lose money, what makes you think you can win? To see your chances of succeeding as a forex trader, here is a checklist for you to see and become one of the elite traders, who make tremendous long term profits. Following are a few ways to lose money. You may wish to change your mind immediately if you are thinking of trying any of them. Do this to avoid losses and continue your forex education!

1. Following a Forex Robot with Simulated Gains - You can apparently achieve success without any effort as promised by these. You are asked to accept their track records simulated going backwards. Your equity will get destroyed by trying them.

2. Day trading and Scalping - Due to the random short term volatility, simply doesn't work. Like the robots, even people selling these always have simulated track records. Many more of these all fall into the category of trying to find someone else to give you success. This does not work in forex markets. Apart from needing a trading edge, you also have to understand ways and reasons of it leading you to success. Let's look at this in detail.

The combination of a simple robust helping you to understand and trade with discipline is what forex trading is about.

You need to know what you are doing to trade with discipline. This translates into having confidence, which you definitely don't get from someone telling you what to do. You get confidence by from your own knowledge and learning.

As you have to keep executing trading signals through losing periods, discipline is hard. This has to be continued till you hit a home run, even when the market is fooling you and taking your money.

What separates out your forex trading system from the 95% losers is your trading edge. You can answer what is your trading edge and how will it help you beat the majority. You don't have one if you don't know what it is.

Few succeed in the simple looking forex trading. These elements are present in the winners' forex trading strategy:

Using simple robust forex trading system

- Having solid grounding in the basics of forex trading

- Knowing exactly why their system will lead them to success

- Having confidence and discipline to stick with their plan

- Knowing only they are responsible for their Forex trading success

You have to stand alone, be confident of your actions and be disciplined to follow your plan in forex trading.

Sounds simple, however it is actually depends on your approach to forex trading - with the right mindset and getting right education. The trader beats himself, rather than the market beating the trader in forex trading.

Learn the basic fundamentals, get a suitable system, become confident, get an edge and be disciplined. Do all of these to enjoy currency trading success.

Never Get Emotional About Trading

Getting emotional in the stock market is the worst thing that can happen to investors. The same goes for Forex traders as well. Seeing paper losses in everyday trade is pretty common. Once to take a decision to buy something and make losses, you still hold on even if situations turn from bad to worse, only because you feel that things might turn back in your favor once again. The main problem here is that, the decision to stick to a losing trade for a long time is an emotional one, since you are in no mood to accept a loss and get out of the trade.

Forex market is largely influenced by the general market and you must always trade on what the indications based on the market are, and not just initiate one since your heart tells you to. At times, you might be so emotionally attached to a given currency in the Forex market, that most of your exposure to the Forex market would be in that particular currency. Nothing wrong with it, as if you have reasonable grounds to believe that the currency will do well, then you will actually profit from the exchange. The 'wrong' thing is opening up a trade in a currency just because your heart tells you to. In the case, if you strongly feel about any given currency, then it's better to check the reality by having the look at what the market is indicating. That will give you a clear picture of whether or not you should trade in that currency.

The basic thing that is needed to be remembered is that once you have initiated a trade, and are incurring paper losses, and by all indications, things are likely to get even worse for you, then it is much better to book losses and come out of it rather than sticking to it till a time you ultimately are able to see some gains from it. Remember, the markets have little room for emotions.

Forex trading is not a win-win situation. Be prepared to lose on some trades as well. That's the precise manner in which the market works. It is not really a question of whether you are right or not, the fact remains that markets move in an unexpected way and they have a knack of surprising people when they least expect it. All the fundamentals and even experience may be thrown into the air when the markets decide to do something.

So just follow the indications that the market gives you. If you feel that after initiating a trade, things are not going the way you had foreseen, book your losses and get out of it. You can invest the amount in some other trade and make good gains rather than sticking to your losing trade.

The Forex Power vs. Forex Assassin Strategy

For those who have an interest in the huge 3 trillion dollars a day foreign exchange market it is common knowledge that to be able to remain on the right side of the Forex market what you require is to constantly discover new plans to minimize your losses and to maximize your profits, and to always adapt so that you can grab any and every opportunity to get a bigger share of the pie.

The Forex Assassin formula and the Forex Power Strategy course are two of the most widely used currency trading tools. Both these tools have received great reviews, but their operating principles are entirely different. As a Forex trader, how would you understand which is the better tool for you? To help you out of your confusion, just read on.

The Forex Assassin formula is designed as a solution to the busy man's problems with forex trading. This tool is ideal for the average 9 to 5 professional who wishes to generate some extra income through Forex dealings but can't muster the time to either monitor the markets throughout the day or study intricate technical formulas, analysis and graphs.

Forex Assassin is a simple and convenient strategy that can be used with little or no understanding of how the market actually works. It normally takes about a quarter of an hour every week to prepare and assign a trading strategy, after which you just have to relax and allow the market to do its work. It is very straightforward, but on the flip side also rather limited, as you are not required to have much understanding of the market. The whole target is to allow the dummy to make limited money by minimizing his chances of loss, which however is not certainly the best way to make the most money.

Conversely, the Forex Power Strategy tool offers a detailed and an in depth course in the dynamics and economics of the market. It takes into account a whole lot of material, and includes all levels of trading. As a result it requires a high investment of your time and attention to make the most of the course and absorb its lessons. So unless you can commit quite some time to it, the Forex Power

Strategy tool is not quite for you. But in return you have the assurance that by the time you complete the course, you will have achieved a better and sounder knowledge of how the market works, and thus your earning potential will be correspondingly higher. But no matter which tool you choose, using either is better than trading just blindly in the market and ending up with huge losses.

CHAPTER 11- UTILIZING THE CORRECT TIMING WHEN TRADING

When you sense a trading opportunity, the deciding factor is to know exactly when to buy. Unfortunately this is the very point at which most loose the plot by timing their entry levels improperly. But here are some basic guidelines to help you at those crucial moments:

Making Proper Use of Support and Resistance

If you try and use the fundamental rule of the share market – "buy low, sell high" – in Forex trading, you'll actually lose money. To understand you need to know how the system of support and resistance works. A support price is a historically tested price at which traders intervene and buy, so as to "support the market". The more this price is tested, the more bankable the support price will be. Inversely, a resistance level is defined as a level at which "prices were resisted from moving any higher". Here too the more this level is tested, the more reliable it becomes.

Why Buy Low and Sell High Doesn't Work

The reason why this traditional wisdom is counterproductive in Forex trading is that if you actually wait for prices to fall, you're going to end up missing some of the best opportunities for making money. Consider: when a currency starts to pick up, what are the chances of its pulling back? What if it doesn't and steadies out? If you keep waiting for a pullback, you could end up never getting in on the trade because most of the changes in currencies occur from new market highs and without any pullback. So if you plan to focus your Forex trade strategy on waiting for an entry at support prices, wake up! You stand to lose out on the most profitable trades. What your Forex trading strategy should target is rather, to "buy high and sell higher" – i.e. you should try and do quite the reverse of what the general crowd is doing. Try and keep a lookout for any breakthroughs in support and resistance, and then sell and buy correspondingly.

It's Gutsy but It Makes Money!

The policy of going against the crowd takes courage to practice. But think over the strategy with a cool head and you shall find it is the most logical thing to do. How often have you heard of traders buying into support, but the market continuing its freefall, breaking the support? And again, haven't you heard tell of the price continuing to soar and never getting to support, thereby making

CHAPTER 12- ADDITIONAL TIPS AND TERMS YOU NEED TO LEARN

The Fluidity of Forex Trading

As one of the benefits of dabbling in the Forex trading market, you will notice that there are many people readily available to trade with you. This is not just because the Forex market offers the large number of transactions per day of any market, though it does that as well, but it is also because Forex trading also provides you with an opportunity to keep your funds very liquid. Because you are trading in currency and because the transactions happen right away, Forex trading is one of the most liquid markets out there. This keeps people interested and tuned in to it. For anyone who is considering the investment in Forex, also know that this liquidity could mean more transactions in a shorter period of time.

The fact that Forex trading markets are so liquid means that you will nearly always have buyers and sellers to trade with if you participate in the market. This liquidity is another way in which Forex is different from other markets around the world. Its uniqueness helps to keep people interested in it.

Although all of the markets in Forex are very liquid and therefore very accessible for most people, it is important to note that the Forex market is particularly liquid in the major markets. Those major currencies are likely to be the place you spend most or all of your time. This includes the USD (United States Dollar), The EURO, the Great Britain Pound and the Yen, though other currencies are just as liquid.

What does this liquidity have to offer to you? There are many benefits, of course, but it does help you to narrow spreads. It also helps to ensure there is some stability in the prices that you deal with. You may be wondering where this type of liquidity comes from. It comes from the banks that provide the necessary liquidity to those who are investors at Forex, including investors, companies, institutions and others who dabble in the market.

The liquidity of the Forex trading market is important for anyone who wants to ensure that they can move money quickly, get to their funds right away and just have less down time between transactions. No matter how much money you would like to invest, knowing that this liquidity exists may encourage you to participate more in the Forex trading market, more so than you might do in other types of markets.

The Pip in Forex

Many terms in Forex trading are important to learn. However, most of the time people can figure out what is occurring since the terms really do lend themselves to their definitions. However, this is not always the case. One of the most commonly asked questions by new traders to Forex is what the pip is. The pip is an important part of the Forex trade and you will see it references through many of the transactions that you make. As you consider all of your trading options, it is best to understand fully this principle before moving on.

In short, a pip is the smallest price chance in that currency exchange rate. In Forex, the market works by trading currency of one country to that of another country. As you can imagine, there are different values here, and that is the overall benefit to trading money. However, there is also the pip to consider. The pip is easier to explain through an example.

For example, recently, the current rate for the Euro and Dollar cross (EUR/USD) was 1.4000. If you added one pip to this, it would equate to 1.4001 for the EUR/USD. In other words, the very last place in the decimal place in this rate is the smallest change in the value of the currency. In this case, the EUR/USD pair has the 1.4001 rate, which is the smallest increase possible.

It is common to see the pips increase by a specific amount, or you may notice that people are saying that the rate went up five pips or ten pips. This simply means that it went up by that amount added onto the end of the number. If the above mentioned cross was at 1.400 and it went up five pips, then it would read EUR/USD equals 1.4000 plus (the lowest increase possible) 0.0005 which equals 1.4005. This is a five pip increase.

How to be a Successful Forex Trader

If you are trading in Forex and you are looking at a chart, you can see this pip change by looking at the very last price bar. It will show you the rate of the increase in the cross. This information can then be used to help you to place additional transactions, or in other words, to help you to buy or sell. The pip is an important part of the currency fluctuation in value and is something to monitor as you are trading.

The Spot Market in Forex

Many aspects of Forex trading are important to note. As you consider the many ways that you can make money on Forex, step back and watch the market play out for some time. In fact, some of the best investors have spent years studying the market so that they could learn how it works and then take that length of education and push it beyond so that they can make money in the market. Whether you spend 10 hours a day staring at data or if you just work at understanding what is happening behind the market, the goal is to learn it. Learn the market inside and out.

One of the things you will want to focus on is the spot market. There are many sectors within the Forex trading marketing, but the spot market is one of the most important for you to take into consideration. This spot market is the area of Forex trading markets that has the largest volume. Volume is a term that shows the amount of trading occurring at the market place. The volume is the number of transactions that are occurring at any given time. Because the spot market does have the most trading it is one of the best places for you to go to invest, too.

In the spot market, you will notice one important factor stands out. The spot market allows for any trades that are made to be settled immediately. For example, if you trade USD for EUR, this transaction, the currency changing hands, happens right at that time, when both parties have agreed to the exchange. This is unlike other markets where there may be a delay in the process of some time. Because the transaction does occur so quickly, people get the instant gratification that they want and they can turn around faster and then resell or re-exchange funds, as they would like to.

It is important to note that although the spot market does trade immediately, this does not mean that the funds are available right at that moment. Rather, there are a few days where the transactions need to transit. This banking time is usually just two days, so long as they are business days. Still, other transactions take far longer to trade. Those who dabble in the Forex market know the importance of trading in this market place for this reason. Fast transactions receive appreciation.

Understanding the Forex Drawdown

In Forex trading, there are many topics to learn about, and many terms you need to know to understand the data presented to you. You see, with Forex, the market changes often and the profits and losses that occur do happen on a regular basis. You need to have the information available to you and be able to understand it fully if you are going to actually make a profit in this type of investment method. One of the terms most commonly asked about is the term drawdown.

A drawdown is an important factor. In fact, it is one you will get to know well when you start out with Forex and you are losing more money than you are making. In a drawdown, you will learn how much money you could lose. In other words, a drawdown is the percentage of funds in an account that you could lose in a situation where there are a streak of losing trades occurring. Another way to explain it is this. A drawdown is the largest loss that your account will take in any given moment or over any period of time. This is a number that you want to keep low, of course in order to be successful in Forex trading.

A streak of losing trades is a term used to describe a losing streak, or a set of consecutive losses that are not profitable to you. Many times, the term drawdown is in use when it is in use to describe a trading system. In other words, as you consider the various trading systems out there, you probably want to know what the biggest loss you can face is if you use that particular trading system. That is not to say that you will lose this amount of money, though. This streak of loses often happens when there is a temporary worsening of the performance of a trading system.

A drawdown is not something you want to happen, but it is something you need to know. If you have $10,000 and you have a 50 percent drawdown, this means that you could lose $5000, which is not small amount of money for the investor. Most drawdown percentages are clearly available to you when you are seeking a trading system. Know what they are and what they represent before you start to get involved in Forex trading.

Should You Go Automated?

Forex trading is nowadays the preferred form of investment for an increasing number of people these days. It is apparent why this is so. As the largest trading market in the world, the Forex market has a steadily growing trading volume, which has risen from around $500 billion to about $2 trillion in the last twenty years. Additionally, since it is not tied to any particular trading floor, it is an unusually liquid market. Operating around the clock also makes it a permanently open market. Thus, since many markets are opening and closing at the same time, one can effectively follow the markets around the world. Both big and small traders are thus being attracted to Forex trading. They enjoy a wide choice of trading strategies based on the various aspects of the foreign exchange rates. Many traders coming into the market find the different things that affect currency exchange rates very attractive for a very simple reason – they can use a wide range to tools when working in this exciting and stimulating market.

Automation is perhaps the greatest influence today on the future growth of the Forex market, as it brings with it more advantages than disadvantages. Manual systems trying to operate in a fast paced and volatile environment bring with them several losses. A simple time delay in buying and selling may cause a row of losses in a manual system and thus cause the trader immense frustration. Automated Forex trading allows trade to be conducted anywhere in the world, in real time, and eliminates the losses seen in manual systems. Operating in a wide range of different currency markets at the same time, without worrying about the time zones of the places concerned, is another advantage that automated Forex trading brings. Sitting in New York at 2 o'clock in the morning, one can conduct business with traders in different countries on the other side of the globe, simultaneously and with great ease. All thanks to automated Forex trading.

Risk management is often a source of worry for traders, but even this is reduced with automated Forex trading. Payments can now be synchronized in real time and this leaves traders satisfied, as opposed to manual trading where there is always uncertainty about payment being made after completion of trade. The automated trading system is developing progressively, and that brings with it hopes that the settlement system will be updated and markets risks will soon cease to exist.

If there is one technology that has advanced by leaps and bounds over the past few years, it is computer technology. Indeed, one hopes that it will continue to grow for many years to come. Most importantly, advances in computer technology spell well for traders who wish to access the best Forex automated trading. Access to technology easily and cheaply from the comfort of the traders' homes means they can manage their own investments with ease. Automated Forex day trading will thus come as a welcome addition to a fully empowered investment vehicle for those in the currency-trading world.

CHAPTER 13- RISKS AND SCAMS

If you are considering an investment into the Forex market, it may be time to take a step back and to really examine if this is the right market place for you to be in. Because of the high level of risk, those without the ability to lose money without losing it all should not be placing their money into this market. One thing that you may hear from time to time is that in Forex, 90 percent of people lose out within their first year. Is it true?

This is the data that is often available. Of all of those who get started in Forex each year, 90 percent of traders will lose all of the money they put into Forex. Only 10 percent of those who get involved in Forex will make money during their first year. This is often a question posed by many new Forex traders because the reality is that you are likely to be in the losing percentage of this transaction.

It is true that many of those who start in Forex will lose their money. There are many reasons for this including a lack of strategy, a lack of training and experience and even arrogance. It is also true that 90 percent of those who invest will lose their money. This refers to each trader that is attempting to make a profit from Forex trading during the first year that they are active in the market place. The numbers do improve, though, for those that stay past this point. In fact, those who are still in the business after one year do not lose money or quit (this is the other 90 percent of the formula) and those that are able to carry on successfully trading are the ones that make up that 10 percent block of people.

There is risk involved in Forex trading. There is no doubt that everyone will lose money from time to time and this is often why so many people do not get involved in this process. However, before you find yourself in a position where you are unable to lose money, be sure that any money that you put into Forex is money that you do not need to pay your bills. It should be money that you can afford to lose. In addition, learn to make the right decisions to reduce your risks here.

Forex Trading Scams

Unfortunately there are some people on the Internet (as well as in real life) that will give their best to take advantage of others. Forex market is very lucrative and tempting opportunity for anyone and therefore most scam artists will use it to lure people into their schemes and steal money from them. That is why I decided to dedicate this entire chapter to forex scams.

Why is it easy to get scammed on the Internet?

1. Because everyone and I mean EVERYONE can purchase a domain name and set up a website for less than $100. Even if they decide

to hire someone to create professional website design for them, they still can get it done for no more than $200 - $300.

2. Most people don't know much about forex market which makes them easy targets for potential scammers as it is very easy to promise dreams and manipulate the numbers and information presented on websites.

3. It is also very easy to hide from public and, once you are scammed, getting your money back can be very difficult or impossible.

The most common schemes relating to forex market are various investment programs, also known as High Yield Investment Programs or HYIPs. The owners of these programs often present themselves as financial experts that can bring unrealistic income through investing in forex, stocks, sports betting, etc. and offer potential investors a chance to profit on their "expertise". People who visit their websites see great opportunity for quick cash and decide to invest money hoping to make a profit. Unrealistic returns they offer are sometimes 200% - 400% within days! But there is a catch. Every investor must wait a certain period of time before he can withdraw money. For example, if the program says the return is 200% within 5 days, it means that if you invest $100, you have to wait 5 days before they "earn" you $200. During that time your investment is locked which means that you can't withdraw even single cent. Of course this time is necessary for owners to "trade with invested money" and "generate profit" to investors. What is really happening nobody knows for sure, but here is most likely scenario: You invest certain amount of money and have to wait for 5 days before you can withdraw any money. During that time, scammers promote their program to find more potential investors.

Scammers also offer you and others commissions for every new investor you bring to their program which makes promotion of their website easy. Each and every one of new investors decides to invest certain amount of money and each and every one of them has to wait 5 days to withdraw any money. After first 5 days scammers usually collect enough money to pay you your profit and to pay their first investors. You and other first investors are happy for your profit and decide to tell everyone you know about this program. The number of investors grows exponentially and the money scammer is receiving grows also.

At one point of time, scammer has enough money to retire young and cannot afford anymore to pay investors their profits and usually HYIP collapses. In this scenario only first investors made profit, while many more that joined this program later lost their money. There are also scenarios where no one gets paid and scammer just collects money, makes empty promises and disappear with his program. Also many scammers return later with new looking program, under different name and scam people again. Some of them even offer realistic income and use that to attract more investors. But one thing you never know about these programs is WHEN it will stop making payments or WHEN it is going to disappear.

You may probably wonder if there are any honest investing programs that really trade with forex or stocks and make profit to their investors. There are, but probably less than 1% of all HYIPs and these programs are usually private and rarely accept new investors. Also their returns are low. If you wonder whether you should invest in HYIPs or not, know this that it is nothing more than a gamble with a lot more chances of losing money and NEVER getting it back!

Besides High Yield Investing Programs there are also other programs, that may seem legitimate, but with only one goal – to take your money. These programs involve various companies and shady brokers who offer foreign currency futures and option contracts, unregistered firms no one even heard about that offer unrealistic return or absolutely no risk involved. Also, be very careful of any "opportunity" that guarantees success as there is no such thing.

ABOUT THE AUTHOR

Laura Evans is an economist, who has dedicated her life teaching at a local university. She specializes in market trend analysis and is considered one of the best in her field.

Laura has earned millions in Forex Trading.

www.ingramcontent.com/pod-product-compliance
Lightning Source LLC
Chambersburg PA
CBHW051237170526
45165CB00004B/1463